THE 5 AM CLUB

THE JOY ON THE OTHER SIDE OF MORNING

MICHAEL LOMBARDI

COPYRIGHT

Disclaimer

As a special Thank You for downloading this book I have put together an exclusive report on Morning Habits.

Learn how to build your own morning routine to achieve increased productivity and less stress. Includes sample morning routines and exclusive tips towards creating your own.

>> You Can Download This Free Report By Clicking Here <<

Kindle 5 Star Books

Free Kindle 5 Star Book Club Membership

Join Other Kindle 5 Star Members Who Are Getting Private Access To Weekly Free Kindle Book Promotions

Get free Kindle books

Stay connected:

Join our Facebook group

Follow Kindle 5 Star on Twitter

Also, if you want to receive updates on Michael's new books, free promotions and Kindle countdown deals sign up to his New Release Mailing List.

The alarm sounds for the first time, 4:55. My instinct, to hit the snooze button, is hindered, as I placed the silly thing across the room, on the chest of drawers, so I would be on my feet before I was even aware of it. It is a hard moment of awareness that this is a change for good, a change the will make me a better person, a change that will change EVERYTHING.

If you are at that same point, that what is just isn't cutting it any longer, then the revelation, the revolution I have to share in the next few pages will also make major change happen in your life. Welcome to the Club. The Five AM Club.

"Early to Bed, Early to Rise Makes a Man Healthy, Wealthy, and Wise."

Ben Franklin, an Honorary Five AM Club member, was speaking from experience, and his precept, fundamentally the same as that of the Club, is that productivity begins with presence. With being awake and aware, and acting accordingly. We succeed when first we set our mind to accomplishment.

By the time I get the alarm silenced, my partner rustles restlessly, finding comfort in a soft pillow, and three more hours of sleep. I took my extra hours last night, to make sure I would be rested enough to make this transition, this shift in paradigm and practice. I hop up and down, as silently as I can, getting the blood flowing throughout my body, and relieving that springiness of slumber. During the hopping, I am digging out my running shorts, socks, and a long-sleeve T-shirt. The morning air will still be brisk, with no sun's rays yet clambering over the horizon, though the glow of its imminence still breathes a promise of warmth soon.

The Five AM Club is more of a grass roots movement than an actual organization, at least so far. The concept is spreading like a veritable wildfire, as these early-rising warriors are taking advantage of an overlooked part of the sidereal cycle, where activity is at a minimum (meaning they are not competing, save with themselves and the growing number of like-minded people who are discovering themselves, their potential, and their objectives head-on in the pre-dawn cool). The advantages these members get are manifold and complex, far beyond just the simple actualization of the extra hours. Together we will identify and address them, and note the impact these advantages have on the lives of Five AM Club members in all their variety.

The first of these advantages is the simplicity and silence that accompanies the early rising. Awakening and immediate activity are associated with the Club, because it is a swift transition from the sleep state to the fully functional state that puts the participant ahead of the rest of the world. It really demands a change in viewpoint, a paradigm shift of philosophical proportion, to move from a steady down state to a steady up state, to go from being just a living organism to a human being truly alive with the potential day already percolating in his or her head.

As I pull on the Tee and skip-hop into the kitchen, the dark silence a pleasant break from the sights and sounds that will soon assail my senses. The alliteration of my thought brings a smile to my face; anyone with even a hint of a creative streak would understand the elation that fills my heart, because a writer lives by the innovation, imagination, and intellect of what he does. As a writer, I can already feel the creative juices beginning to flow. I grab an orange as I hit the door, headed out on a pre-dawn run. It is striking Five AM exactly as I leave the building, already reaching trotting speed. I will be at a full run within a hundred yards of my front door. Good Morning, World.

The origins of the Five AM Club is less a cultural outgrowth than the intensely dedicated founders who simply rediscovered the ancient concept of 'Early to Bed, Early to Rise" made famous more than two hundred thirty years ago, by a guy you might have heard about. (Ben Franklin). But these modern Morning Glories are taking the concept to a whole new height, hitting the ground on the run first thing, and getting the day off on the right foot, by making the morning routine not just about accomplishing the basics, but about being fully present from that very first second. Like Parkour disciples, they are learning as they go, and loving every minute of it.

Another tenet therefore of the Club, is that the present is a malleable fluid state, where the decisions of the present can alter and shift, pouring reality into a predefined framework of will. This is to say that our existence in a Five AM Club lifestyle is one of concrete action following concrete action with determination and tenacity, to accept the things that are, but alter the situation that is, to create the future that should be.

Action is the lever by which we alter the course of events to move from what might have been to what we wish to be.

- - -

There is a different feeling, to be clicking along at a gripping pace while starting up the internals, kind of like the pre-start of a rocket launch protocol, the rapid intake and exhalation of the crisp morning air is an igniter. The actual process of the run is giving my mind the time it needs to get started, and the oxygen-rich blood pumping into my brain is like gasoline on a grass fire. By the time I am headed home, my brain is already filled with energy, awake and afire with the sheer joy of life. Oh, and endorphins. Those are good, too.

Ingrained in the Five AM Club concept is an immediacy of action, a constant and driving awareness of time that perhaps has been missing in previous mindsets. And a mindset is truly what one is talking about, when he or she discusses the Club. It's an individualized process, one that can include others, but that is a personal accountability mechanism. No one is going to turn on your morning alarm for you, or call you on missing the mark. But an internalized drive becomes instilled, and reinforced with every success.

It isn't whether you succeed, but when you do, that matters.

In the regular world, the conditions and situations in which we become enmeshed are not of our express doing, but are reflections of the will of the hundreds of people around us that we allow to impact us. A Five AM Club worldview rejects the input of others as final arbiter, and instead exerts the sheer act of choosing actions as the means to take control. So it is, if you will, an extension of the concept of intent, that what one pursues with passion and persistence becomes reality over the passage of time.

Padding back to the apartment, I pass a half dozen homes that are currently for sale. One of my objectives, one of the focuses that keep me working the Five AM Club strategy, is clearing my credit problems, so I can buy a place of my own. Like a marathon racer, I have learned to be patient; some objectives are not accomplished immediately, that they can take a long time to achieve. I turn on my computer, the coffee maker, and hit the shower. By the time I am out, clean and ready for the day, so will be the coffee and the computer. I pack my evening clothes into my bike's saddlebags, and dress for the brisk ride to the bus station. I have the laptop set up on a Bistro table; I surrendered my office-style chair in trade for more time away from the keyboard. By deciding to stand to check the social sites and the local and national news from that vantage point, my patience has become tied to the fatigue of standing… that means I necessarily don't spend all the hours I used to updating, and offering 'likes' to things. I think it increases the value of them, to know for myself that I just don't click in because I can, but because it meant enough to me to do so. Breakfast is light, just a bagel with cream cheese and an apple, along with the coffee, and I am ready to go before the clock strikes six.

One of the constants that the Five AM Club members uniformly deal with is the darkness of the hour. Whether east coast or west, whether in Daylight Savings Time or Standard Time, North or South, that hour is fundamentally pre-dawn. So those times, those precious early minutes, are far more intimate, more individual, than later or even earlier hours. Midwestern farmers have the standard lifestyle that is probably the closest analog to the lifestyle of the Club members. The primary difference between them is that the Farmer is serving the needs of the crops or the herd; Clubbers are acting on a level of informed selfishness; the drive they choose to respond to are their goals and objectives, their own focus and intent. It can be arguably too self-focused, so most of the Five AM Club members have discovered that their goals often are easier to be motivating if they serve others along the way. Like the recent Lincoln advertisements have it, it's about taking care of something else, while you're taking care of yourself that makes the difference.

Doing something for your self is selfish and unproductive. Doing something to improve yourself is selfless, and extends your existence into the lives of others in a way that offers them the chance to improve as well. The Five AM Club lifestyle is opposed to the former, and embraces all the potential of the latter.

Taking on a life that is mentally engaging, physically demanding, and spiritually uplifting is a challenge. It would be more difficult for me if I had stayed plugged into local and national television, so I chose to disconnect from the regular news sources, and limit my input of negative data to that early-morning perusal of the headlines. I don't want to appear negligent or ignorant of the goings-on of the world. But I do prefer to restrict the negative energy as much as I can.

When I am done with my coffee, and the email stream has been managed, I put the computer on snooze mode, and take care of the physical needs of an apartment. Feed the fish, wash the dishes in the sink, pick up the clothes in the bedroom, and pull up the bedclothes, making it presentable. Since that part of the morning doesn't take much thought, I take that time and put in earbuds, listening to the audio book I started yesterday. It's an ongoing conversation, if you will, between the author and I, and regardless of what title, the point of the exercise is to challenge and test my own thought processes. Does the work have to be a dry, non-fiction self- help work? Not necessarily, but for my time's value, it most usually is.

Being a member of the Five AM Club doesn't require a membership card, member service number, or anything else to define you beyond your desire to make this change in lifestyle. As a matter of fact, there are a lot of honorary members throughout history who, without having the snappy name, were already taking some of the major tenets of the philosophy to the logical extreme, living every day in the moment, seeking the same level of personal accomplishment and perfection. Bruce Lee. Nikola Tesla. Einstein.

But there is now a more significant change in the Club. Not only does one want to accomplish and succeed in endeavor, one also wants to achieve a heightened success in physical accomplishment and business, finance, and spirituality. It isn't mumbo-jumbo, but rather a quantum change in the success platform of the past. It isn't about doing your best; it is about being YOUR best. Firing on all cylinders. Watching all horizons. Truly, a centralized global view. If one is the best, he cannot be less than that in all areas of life. It is a mind-blowing experience, when one awakens to the realization that one can truly make better, be better, in every subcategory and niche of existence. And it gets even more mind-boggling when one begins to experience successes on more than one front.

I'm done with the menial tasks of life, have already begun my day, and it is only six fifteen in the morning. The business aspect of my life won't kick into gear until nearly nine, so that leaves me time to begin my preparation for the whole day. I pack my workout gear into the backpack, check the air in the bike tires, and flip the laptop back out of slumber. I check email, not for the pleasure of seeing messages from friends, but to verify the links to the news sources I will want to go over before the market opens, and the workday begins. I do note two new jobs have dropped into the hopper, so I quickly prioritize them with the rest of the work I have on the burners. I also verify the auto-pay for my bills have been enacted for this month, and the balance I have left over. I plan on going out to dinner tonight, and to make a transfer to savings of the remainder. That down payment for the house has to come from somewhere. After that, I shut down the laptop again, this time shutting it completely down, as I have to make the trek to the office, and that will be a bike and bus trip of about an hour, too long for the laptop battery, and besides, I won't be looking at it until I get to the office. While it is powering down, I am setting up the MP-3 player for the bike ride, getting the earbuds in place. I have prepped a half hour of energizing and positive music with and advanced beat, perfect for the bike ride, and a 30-minute audio book, recommended by another Five AM Club member. At precisely seven AM, I am on the bike and headed toward the station.

Five AM Club members only begin their day at that hour; because they reach that deep level of intention and activity so early, they achieve their goals and objectives at a higher rate, and to a deeper level, than their competitors who do not. Whether the goals are manifested in greater financial success or not is more a factor of their desires than of the value of their actions. Indeed, it is a shift in mind set that moves from measuring success by the dollars per hour, and instead to a consistent pattern of accomplishment. The ones who win are those that actively seek to do, not just those who broker financial benefit from their endeavors.

Yet the growing resume that includes measured and intentional successes does lead to greater compensation. Though it is not a direct focus, financial success is a derivative of the reported effort, and consistent accomplishment leads to compensation. That's important.

Communicated Consistent Accomplishment leads to Compensation.

Note that isn't just that one accomplishes tasks, but that one is able to confidently express his successes, so that others are aware of them. There is a thin line, however, between doing something positive and then conveying that reality, and doing the positive thing only to be acknowledged for it. The former is a Five AM Club tenet; the latter is 'business as usual, tit for tat, quid pro quo', and far off the mark.

About the time I have pedaled to the station, my playlist has come to an end, and I get the eBook cued up. Since there is always the possibility to learn something, to hear something really revolutionary in the book, I pull a small notebook out of my backpack, and after locking my bike into the train's rack, I press play. I have to admit some days the short ride downtown lulls me back to sleep, a fifteen to twenty minute powernap kind of doze, but the words of the eBook are pumping then directly into my subconscious. So whether actively chasing new information, or letting something perhaps that is a variation on old themes burn into my cortex, either way the ride rejuvenates me.

Disembarking, I cruise the rest of the way in to the office, appreciating the cardiovascular boost of the bike. It is going to be an awesome day. Already has been, so far.

Another aspect of the Five AM Club that reaps a lot of benefit is in the area of volunteerism. Since the lion's share of the work that members need to accomplish for their own goals is accomplished earlier in the day, there is a considerable amount of time left over for personal sacrifice, giving back in kind for the benefits of a good life. Direct, personal work like serving in a homeless shelter food kitchen is only the beginning. What is most fascinating is that once you delve into the concept of volunteering your personal time, there appear opportunities to do what you do best, for the betterment of humanity. Perhaps you are an accountant; there are a lot of folks who desperately need assistance in getting their finances together, from a tax standpoint, or even learning the basics of a budget, and how to manage what they earn. Or perhaps you are in construction; Habitats for Humanity has a constant need for those who can swing a hammer or run electrical wiring. It is in these moments, when the power of personal advancement turns to serve humanity as a whole, that the appeal to join the Five AM Club becomes more than just a nice idea. It becomes a campaign that could change everything, if we all gave back in kind. Or maybe a little more.

After the routine morning meeting with the other members of our team, I dive into the work, and for the next three hours, I am lost in the routine of it. My mind, engaged fully, is oblivious to my physical needs, and I would sit at the desk without taking a break, but my cellphone alarm breaks up the day, by reminding me to get up and go at least once an hour. I use different musical tones, so that I am able to know how far through the day I am with each trigger.

When the alarm goes off, I silence it, and immediately stand up. Smokers in my office call it my "Nope" breaks, because it is analogous to their "Smoke" breaks. But instead, I head to the staircase, and get in a couple of laps down to the ground floor and back, or I go to the upper floor of the parking structure to put some ground beneath my feet for a while, or I just go out the restroom to do what is natural. The point is at least once an hour I am mobile, getting the aerobic systems and cardiopulmonary systems moving again, driving metabolism. By the time the third alarm has sounded, I am ready for lunch, and I am going again.

In certain ways, the Five AM Club concept is a launching pad for an adventurous life. Many proponents of the Club are physical overachievers, testing the limits of their bodies and of human experience, practitioners of Parkour and BASE Jumping, Marathon and Iron Man competitions. They press their bodies as hard as they push their minds. The Club is their mainstay of life, and they are seeking to experience it to the extreme.

Making a decision to be and act conclusively and without regret or reservation puts the Membership into the top one percent; perhaps not in income, but in consecutive and consistent accomplishment, measurable metrics in any category.

As a Five AM Club practitioner, I am adventurous in a lot of ways that go beyond exercise and study. In my work area, there are probably fifty locally owned little restaurants, and as many national chain and franchised locations. Each day I don't pack a lunch, I try a different one of these local places, in part to support my local economy, and to test the gastronomic waters, as it were. Some of the places are quaint, charming, and extremely generous in portions and quality; some are not worth the time of day. Still, without experimentation there is no discovery, so the process continues. Today is a Thai restaurant, and I am not disappointed. Chalk one up for the good guys.

Although in a lot of ways the Five AM Club concept is isolationist and a solo sort of lifestyle, there are actually a great number of moments of camaraderie and collective acknowledgement. Just in the past few months, dozens of Five AM Club- dedicated websites and in general a great many more personal advancement sites have begun to provide support and outreach to the de facto membership. Social interaction concerning running sites, restaurants and coffee houses that cater to the Club, as well as meet ups and other collective activity options are being exercised across the country. As much as we all appreciate personal achievement, we all also relish acknowledgment for our successes, as well as encouragement to press on in the face of temporary setbacks and outright opposition. One might say that the Five AM Club is a collective community of creative and compelling compatriots, all chasing the challenge of accomplishing the personally possible.

The restaurant is busy but speedy, and I am back on the bike, headed back for the afternoon at the office. I take a few moments to verify my evening's schedule. I check with a coworker on social media, and ensure all is on as we had planned. Getting back to the office, I carry the bike up the stairs for the extra cardio, and drop back into the routine for the afternoon calls. It's a Monday, so the calls are all fairly humdrum, no major drama.

Life in the Five AM Club is embraced by people from a lot of different walks of life, and while some find themselves drifting back into the old routines, the establishment of new habits and new ways of going about daily activities can help anchor in the new, and put an end to the old. The transition from home-based telephone systems to a cellular-only lifestyle is a great example of something that embraces the Club, and helps put an end to the old, traditional, and dying way of doing things.

When your friends, co-workers, and business associates all have you on speed dial, you tend to live in the moment, take advantage of a faster life pace, and embrace life as a whole, not just a part of your life. The people in your life are your family, and your family becomes a bigger part of your life. Indeed, as you expand your life to take in the new hours, and the new way of thinking, your understanding of the role of the individual in humanity takes on new meaning, new impact. Your life is your own, but the experiences you have belong to the world, belong to human awareness. We are more than the sum of our parts.

It's the end of the day, and the staff is departing on its way to the various homes and dwellings. I take the bike to the street, and in moments I am whizzing toward the hospice near the city hospital. A couple of hours visiting the hospice center, where I have made friends with a few people dealing with late-stage cancer really helps me keep life in perspective. Then, before I head back to the apartment, I am going to check out the jump site for this weekend's BASE jump, a building on the north side with a pretty challenging wind signature. Personally, I haven't the courage to make the actual jumps, but I am an accomplished parachute packer and the team's photographer. I will be looking for key vantage points, and figuring out how to install the cameras in advance of the jump without threatening the mission by tipping off the authorities. The city I live in still does not allow for nor permit such activity, so we have to be expedient and efficient to avoid detection. Even so, the thought of the jump is pretty exhilarating, and by the time I am heading back home, I see the whole experience for what it is, another data point in human existence, another proof for the ages that anything is possible, that we can accomplish what we set our minds to do.

I stop and pick up a few items at the corner market, and a particularly appetizing steak for the hibachi. IT is too nice to cook indoors tonight; the little charcoal burner will be perfect. The sun is sliding into the bay to the west, and another perfect day is coming to a close. I pedal back up the hill, my legs burning from the effort, and I climb the steps, bike on shoulder, backpack as a counterbalance.

If it hasn't become apparent yet, the Five AM Club lifestyle is perfectly suited for a greener, safer, more energetic and inclusive world than any other lifestyle basis. Anyone can pursue their own particular passion and still embrace the collective and individual tenets of simplicity, presence, and accomplishment. But as we come to the end of the basics, we will spend the next few pages talking about the longer-term implications of a Five AM Club life, and not only what it entails, what is expected of those who hold to its core, but the reasons that a Club life demands a kind of propagation, a need to expand the concepts to others, and to bring about for others the same epiphany that the practitioner has undergone. This is how a good thing gets better.

As the hibachi coals reach uniformity, I place the steak above them gently, purposefully. The vegetables I microwaved, more to ensure a common cooking time, not because I disdain them boiled or steamed. As it sends up savory aromas, I think back on the day, what I have done, what I have read and heard. I begin to correlate the reality I have now, with the one I am endeavoring to achieve.

Little baby steps, honestly, but as I partake of the meal for one, I can see the horizons before me, the objectives I have yet to accomplish, and I am satisfied that I am on course, on tempo to achieve what I am seeking to accomplish in my lifetime.

The 'UNOFFICIAL' Five AM Club Credo

The concept of starting one's day in the pre-dawn quiet isn't something to be codified, qualified, or put in a framework. Still, for a booklet like this, some framing makes for an easier conversation, so below are the fundamentals of a Five AM Club philosophy. In between each of the five premises, I will explain for each the five ways that Joy can be discovered through this journey to the Other Side of Morning, where accomplishment and success reside in harmony with health, wealth, and wisdom.

I will start each day, awake and alert and active, at Five AM local time

It sounds simple, doesn't it? One day, anyway. It seems that the challenge of the Five AM Club isn't the doing, it is the doing again. And again. So the joys that come from that one decision, made again and again, are joys that are deeper than those warm blankets you were snuggled in, and the accomplishment of the difficult over the long haul speaks louder than that alarm clock.

Good morning, Sun Shine.

The Joy of Accomplishment.

There is a difference between saying you will accomplish, and accomplishing it. Still, there is a kind of commitment one makes when he puts words to his objective, because stating it is the essence of exerting one's will on the world. A commitment to even a simple thing like awakening at a certain hour, and beginning your day upon arising is a first, an accomplishment of a promise, even if it is to one's self. There is power in commitment to anything. So though it may seem a little thing to you to make this a reality, you have already made an action, a decision made real. You have reached, if in a tiny way, the objective of the Five AM Club. You made a change in your life. One that can and will be good for your entire life. But do note that the statement includes a continuous nature… starting EACH day, not just the first. So do you see the exciting reality in the challenge? It tasks you with that same enthusiasm, that same sense of accomplishment and endeavor, for the rest of your life. Amazing, really.

The Joy of Alternatives

If you haven't grasped yet the concept of immediacy, this would be a great time to open your mind, and accept that it is in this very moment that you have an infinity of alternatives before you, and that the staggering and awe-inspiring concept is that each floating instant, every moment we live and breathe, that vast field of opportunities lies before us. The more open you become to the possibilities, the more humbled and aware you become. And the decision to awaken early provides even more options than if you slept away those extra hours. It can only bring smiles to your face when you consider all you can really do to change things, right here, right now.

The Joy of Awareness

Getting your day going earlier, and at a precise moment of your choosing delivers another kind of Joy. The silence and solitude of an early and intentional rising brings coherence and clarity to your thoughts, a level of dedication that is made manifest in those moments of decision, when you take the bull by the horns, and choose your course for the coming hours, still realizing that you are in complete control of the hours and their fulfillment. Even if your decision is to focus on a single objective, or fill your day with myriad tasks, it is ultimately the peaceful dedication of your heart to the day's activities that sets your course, and defines your existence. You are in control, and that is powerful.

The Joy of Adaptation.

As powerful as intention is, our desires do not always happen as we expect, and we don't ever fully comprehend how the interaction of other souls, other seekers, can impact what we are working toward. So it is that we learn, by experience if not by teaching, that in most cases, the cleverest derive their concepts from the actions of others, or by happenstance. Put another way, ingenuity is the byproduct of unbridled action. As Thomas Edison said, he did not fail over a thousand times in his search for a way to create electric light, he instead discovered over a thousand ways to NOT create electric light. The early-morning awareness that our efforts lead toward success, but are not specifically deemed to be THE breakthrough day, lets us appreciate and enjoy every day with the same wonder and surprise at its outcome.

The Joy of Awareness

If you have ever had a task to accomplish that defined you, that consumed all your thoughts until you had finished it, you know this joy. Children often experience this when they do well on a test they thought they might fail, or create something artful that others appreciate and respond to. Awareness can be major, serious, and demanding, or it might be the fruition of a natural skill or gift; success is achieved when action is guided to accomplishment. We know our purpose when we engage with the world in order to achieve it, regardless of the effort, the work, and the challenge it will take to complete.

I will only worry about doing what I can, to the best of my ability

Perfection is not a human trait, it is a human dream. With every decision comes contradiction and opposition. The joys of becoming worry-free far outweigh the seemingly dire protectionism that worry is intended to elicit. Still, the success of any individual in overcoming the human tendency to dwell on and attempt to fix problems, real or imagined, is a herculean effort, that in itself should bring satisfaction. These joys therefore are particularly sweet, because they represent successful growth in action.

The Joy of Rising

There is an old saw, that relates that it isn't the number of times a person is knocked down that defines the success, but the number of times you get back up. While some might suggest there is an air of masochism to it, there is a euphoria one can experience when he or she stands up again, after recognizing and acknowledging, but not accepting a defeat. The real measure of success is the amount of learning each such setback creates, and how that learning is applied in subsequent altercations. Accomplishment is the persistent overcoming of interim obstacles and failures, and it is absolutely imperative that a Five AM Club practitioner sees the failures and setbacks only as a backdrop for the next assault on those objectives. In ancient times, the crowds would roar each time the fallen gladiator would regain his footing, shake of the pain and injury, and rejoin the fray. So it is for we who aspire for success. We must take the affliction that the world tosses at us, learn from the injuries, and just keep getting back to our feet. Every journey begins with the first steps, and ends only when we abandon them. The successful never cease to advance.

The Joy of Renewal

Sometimes the course, which we set for ourselves, is more difficult or out of sync with the universe. WE can slam our heads against the impermeable, only to end up with a headache and perhaps blood, sweat, and tears seemingly wasted on a strategy that simply is not producing success. The fortunate aspect is that, as my grandfather would say, there is more than one way to "skin a cat". But that seeming waste is actually a harsh schoolmaster, because sometimes it isn't the strategy that fails, but the willingness of the universe for that success to come at that point, or by that method.

Praise be, we have the chance, at any point, to start over again, to choose a different set of parameters, to make a new assault on the heights. There is a cleansing of the heart and mind when we can accept an initial ascent may not be our final one, and that our strategy, or mechanics, our entire plan may have to be reworked. And the Joy follows when we can see the freshness, the lessons learned in application. This is ultimately the result of the willingness to accept the ultimate definition of responsibility for all of one's actions and inactions, to analyze and change course appropriately.

The Joy of Reward.

Most tasks are difficult, and usually have to be divided into segments to be accomplished. Sometimes, the number of segments is daunting, and the need to appreciate the routine necessary to accomplish the task arises. So when those times come, like when one is trying to finish a college degree program, but the classes seem to drag on and on....or when one has to make three hundred more quilting blocks to finish that charity project... one need so enable the Repetition's reward. Throughout this book, I have referred to benchmarking, and this is precisely how best to put such to work.

As all one can ever do is make the attempts at success, count the number of times a particular task needs to be done, and set up appropriate awards for oneself based on accomplishing hard, solid numeric objectives. Then, as you achieve each of these benchmarks, acknowledge to yourself that success, and fulfill that award with all enthusiasm. You may be aware of how well you are progressing, but taking this extra step and offering Repetition its own reward not only reinforces the objective, but it recognizes how challenging it is just to make the effort, and how that challenge is worthy of recognition. Good Job!

The Joy of Realization

Success will come when it is deserved and accepted. It is one thing to see an objective coming into view, to see the finish line on a project or a goal, but it is far more gratifying to embrace and accept that achievement. Our world does much to try to downplay any individual efforts as being integral to success; we want the measure of a man to be how much he gives away of his efforts, not how much he takes credit for. SO, as it is with all great individuals, one should share in the recognition of the efforts of others, but one should at least for themselves accept and embrace their own efforts and sacrifice made to achieve the accomplishments. In other words, it is perfectly acceptable to raise your arms in victory, and to say, "I DID THIS!"

The Joy of Resolution

The move from idea to reality is often fraught with many forms of opposition. From the basic ennui of a system that has not been challenged before, to vested interests from people who are benefitting from an antiquated process, to the sheer fear factor, those who are overly concerned about the impact of change, the Five AM Club strategist not only learns to define, but to defy, those forms of external challenge, Accomplishment is achieving in the face of opposition, and the person who develops the tenacity to continue when they are tested are the ones who will write the rules going forward. There is a satisfaction in shutting down a naysayer, and something even more rewarding about completing things that others said was impossible to accomplish.

I will set for myself attainable & progressively challenging goals

For most of us, goal setting sounds and usually is a grueling process, because we most often confuse a goal with a wish, an objective with a desire. Holding, as a Five AM Club member, specific agenda points that are associated with particular points in time give us not only a measurable way to experience movement toward accomplishment, we offer for ourselves incentives, benchmarks, by which we can visualize and experience the little successes along the way that feed the imagination, and warm the heart with accomplishment.

The Joy of Effectiveness

Goals are promises with an expiration date. If we hold to our singleness of mission, coupled with our immediacy of action and our strategy for success, we can experience the measured forward progress when it happens. A person who stares at the mountain ahead misses out on the beauty of the current position. In other words, if you are focusing on the destination, it is difficult to feel the incremental advances. But if you have your eye on the activity of today, you can feel the tangible movement, the inexorable motion toward the goal. Setbacks will be more keenly felt, it is true, but such only acts as a catalyst to making the changes needed to make the next steps forward more assuredly, more truly toward the goal.

The Joy of Effort

Biologists tell us that as we exert effort physically, the body creates pleasant experience through the release of endorphins, very addictive and pleasure-creating chemicals that reinforce the physical activity as pleasant and the feelings created by the effort are amplified positively. So it is that the very process of moving toward our objectives is in a way its own reward. Something need not be easy to obtain for it to be a pleasure to achieve. Attainment doesn't mean simplicity or ease in accomplishment, but means we go after that objective with not only a mind and a will to achieve, but also the determination to follow the actions through necessary to make it happen. And Joy results simply from making the attempt with every fiber of our being. It feels good to make the effort itself, whether the effort ends in success or learning experience.

The Joy of Edification

One does not exist solely in a robotic, automaton way, but instead seeks to be recognized and rewarded, from within and without, when we make advancement. For this reason, each measured and accepted achievement should be praised as a stepping-stone toward the objective. Building up our routines, our works toward our ultimate goals, we create a positive and supportive environment in which successes become the norm, and yet the learning experiences become acceptable, and the setbacks are seen only as launch pads for fresh alternatives and necessary paradigm shifts. One is either building up or one is tearing down, and the Five AM Club values embrace the edification process, heaping positive uplifting messages upon successes, and creative and helpful revisions in cases of setback. The building of a healthy and optimistic psyche is every bit as necessary as the accomplishment of the physical objectives.

The Joy of Expectation

Some may call the expectation of success to be a thing of arrogance, but in reality, the assumption of success is necessary to bridge the gap between what is probable, and what is possible. To hold a view that what you are hoping to accomplish exists only in the realm of the impossible is one sure way to assure you will not succeed. So to not only avoid the heartache of creating an adverse foregone conclusion, it is essential that we expect our performance will exceed all obstacles, if the impossibility that others foresee. It is crucial that we realize that the intent of others and their external expectations are not sufficient to keep us on point, so personally-set benchmarks are more valuable, our own expectation of success more powerful.

The Joy of Exaltation

It is often said that unless you learn to toot your own horn, no one will let you into the band. Our American culture, formerly so self-assured and confident would proudly extol our own value, or own successes. In recent years, however, there has been such a push to create cultural commonality, that people have in many cases either forgotten how to be gracious in success and respectful in victory, or have simply succumbed to the I idea that corporate, collective successes are the only ones of value. The truth is, communication of accomplishment leads to credible compensation, and unless you are willing to embrace your successes, the value thereof is diminished. The euphoria of achieving an objective, of reaching a goal, should be infectious, and drive others to desire their own success. Indeed, it is a tragedy when we hear of persons whose success only comes to fruition after their death, or their reward is held back by social pressure. It is terrific to share in a joint effort, and give credit to the whole team. But it is wrong to undermine your own success by giving away the responsibility, the credit for work done well,

I will study and learn from successful people in all walks of life

From the cradle to the grave, we are always susceptible to learning, to discovering new information and acting upon it. This uplifting and educational aspect of life is a focus of the Five AM Club concept, one that not only offers new vistas to explore, but new means to accomplish our objectives, new tools for defining our existence. Whether the education comes from direct experience, or from the tutelage of others, every lesson learned is a stair step toward greatness. Here are five of the unearthed joys of Club membership under this basic tenet.

The Joy of Visualization

Like the development of the microscope and the telescope, both in the micro- and macrocosm, we discover the more we know, the more there is to learn. In just such a fashion, the pathways to achieve success have common themes, but have many facets, and the more you study, the more you see there is to be learned. In particular, the ability to project from the present to that place where our freedoms really exist offers utter joy in our development of a success mentality. We can begin to overcome the obstacles in our way, once we lift our eyes from the specific challenge, and see the course beyond the difficulty. Much as the technique used to learn to ride a bicycle, once one take his or her eyes from the handlebars, and projects to where the bike will be soon, the balance becomes natural, the adjustments less exaggerated. We move from fearful nearsightedness to fearless farsightedness.

The Joy of Validation

It is often said that Great Minds Think Alike. This may be because great ideas derive from common understanding, but it also tends to be because younger Great Minds learn from other, older ones. There are conditions, circumstances, that are at least very similar, if not completely repetitive, and those that survive and recall those conditions go on to be considered great minds, having learned how to resolve those situations. So it is with great pride and joy one can revel in those times when one's own successes validates these older provisions, because it reflects our own wisdom and philosophy.

They say that emulation is the highest form of flattery, and perhaps it is, but emulation of the things learned vicariously, without having to succumb to the same pitfalls and challenges that others have endured by paying attention and studying their course, is not only a reflection of wisdom, it is also evidence of humility. Our willingness to follow instruction does not make us weak, but rather emboldens us in areas of experimentation in life, because we have learned the basics, and have set our feet on the selfsame pathway to greatness as our mentors and heroes.

Each time we find ourselves accomplishing on that basis therefore, we add credibility to our cause.

The Joy of Vindication

Of course, no two situations are identical, but many have complementary conditions. Sometimes we must strike out in a new direction, blaze our own course, in order to overcome some new challenge for which there appeared no precedent, no means to aggressively emulate others. In those moments, it is our tenacity, our ability to stick to an agenda that is our own, that will either offer a learning point, where we must correct our course, or will offer our thought processes a vindication, an internal proof of concept, and give us a level of pride unparalleled.

Ultimately, all education, all learning leads to these seminal moments of decision-making where the decisions are all ours, and our success or failure falls squarely on our shoulders. And make or break, win or lose, it is those moments that define us as arrogant and untrainable, or humble and solemn learners. Successes by a trial of fire.

The Joy of Verification

Every successful person begins as a hopeful one. By listening to our mentors, reading the works of our champions and personal idols, we begin the process of becoming more than the sum of our parts. Again there is a platitude that Leaders are Readers, and that Readers are Leaders. The truth is perhaps more broad than this, but at its core, this is absolutely true. Unless one is willing to bend his or her will to adhere to what we are taught, we are doomed to constantly repeat and re-instigate the mistakes and errors of the past.

Even with the highest hopes in the world, there must be external proof that our objectives have succeeded, some measurably identifiable metrics that hold as evidence for others of our accuracy, effort, and achievement. So when that first, second, or final evidence becomes available, there is yet another means of experiencing joy. You did it. It is finished.

The Joy of Vocalization

Akin to the Exaltation in the previous section only in terms of the content, the joy of which I speak now is that capability to share with others the ways in which you accomplished your own objective, achieved excellence in our own process, and how you not only accumulated success, but how that success has impacted your life from that point onward. One of the world's greatest fears is that of public speaking, but the Five AM Club member lives in a fearless environment, and though it is daunting, the very need to share your message helps overcome the fear, and soon, the message is so compelling you have no choice but to share what you have learned, how you have succeeded. As it was with the fear of acting in the first place, the desire to share compels one to take personal and immediate action to convey the simplicity and the audacity it takes to accomplish. Soon, it becomes as natural as the effort to succeed was in the first place.

I will be present and aware in all life processes I experience

From the moment we are personally aware until our last conscious moment, life is a limited-time offer. We don't get do-overs, and we can't go back. Ever. So the best we can hope for is a fully aware passage through life, getting all we can accomplish and all we can ever hope for achieved in our finite framework. Even in this solemn vein, there abound joys we haven't touched on yet, so hang on, these are arguably the most poignant ones of them all.

The Joy of Intimacy

While we are surrounded by people throughout our lives, the Five AM Club has set itself apart by time, and are in a unique position, wherein what they each wish to accomplish individually is also that for which they all strive collectively. There is strength in sharing a common objective of personal success and growth, even as each pursues that objective in his or her own way. We are bound together by the same sacred desire, to accomplish. That is something that brings a level of vulnerability, because the Club offers to let us share our goals with others, and thereby increase our chances at success.

The Joy of Immediacy

Throughout this book we have talked about living in the moment, of keeping our heads in the game at every play, every moment we are engaged. The elation we feel when we consider what we have accomplished, what we will achieve in the future, is a result of a very tangible engagement with the very essence of time. In this moment, we are no longer constricted by hours, minutes, even seconds. We can contact the future and the past through our mental discipline, and we can feel in advance the wonder and adulation that our later success will bring. All points in time conjoin in this moment, in the now.

The Joy of Identity

Another staggering kind of joy is the realization and awareness of our unique nature. No one else can be us. No one else can experience the life, the challenges, and the success of our life other than ourselves. The magnitude of that reality can be more than we can really comprehend, because we often surround ourselves with so many others. But no one else has our demeanor or perspective. In being one of a kind there is a wonder and pride that certainly can be experienced by no one else. We are the only ones who can be us.

The Joy of Ingenuity

Our perspective on the world gives us each a unique paradigm, a specific viewpoint on all that is before us. When we consider the present, the future, it is in this specialized perspective that we can take the options and variables, make them our own, and act accordingly. The greatest of minds hide their sources the best, and it is simply our decision how communal or how isolationist our life will be. It is in the discoveries that one can make choosing to live this Five AM Club lifestyle that changes our perspective, gives us the keys to our own success, and drives us to a new level of experience, awareness, and ability. WE are the genie in the bottle, the puppeteer behind the marionettes. It is our will, and our choices that define or alter the course of life.

The Joy of Immortality

Living in the present moment is the purview of children the world over, and re-learning this skill is a necessity in developing the Five AM Club mentality. Tomorrow is an eternity away, the past is infinitely behind us, but the complete openness of this precise moment offers us the opportunity again to live each moment as a separate infinity, a finite block of the infinite, wherein we can interact, love, breath, live and express our emotion and our will into the world like the blowtorch of action it is. The pure fascination with the passage of time affords us that childlike wonder, that willingness to be fearless, because we honestly don't know what the next moment will bring. WE find ourselves in a passion, staring into the eternal, daring to make the changes in life that will alter the eternal, and realizing that the power that resides in one of us resides in each of us. There is hope left in the world, but it is up to us, the life members of the Five AM Club, to grasp our joy in the morning, well before the rest of the world wakens from its slumber, and embrace the Morning from the Other Side.

CONCLUSION

Some may take a look at this book, and see philosophical mumbo jumbo, not realizing its impact on the participant's life. Others will read this, nod, and say it is for someone else, for a different kind of person from himself or herself.

But the real truth is that this book is an eye-opener, a beginning salvo in a worldwide revolution. We challenge you to take the Five AM Club challenge, and give the process itself a month of concentrated effort, customizing its basics for our own purposes. Whether you have a prime objective in mind or not, acting on the basic premises will give you hours of more productivity. The opening of your mindset to new potentials, the recommendation to learn from other successful people, and a clear understanding on what kind of life is ahead of you are all going to bring other changes, unexpected changes, to your life.

Don't take my word for it. Follow these five steps, and you will see what we are proposing for what it is, a life changing series of actions that will open the world to you in unexpected ways, and with life-altering consequences.

    1. Set your alarm for 4:50, but set it up across the room.

    2. Commit to getting up at the first setting, and hop or jump for five minutes after you get out of bed to shut it off.

    3. Go. Get out of the house. Whether a bike ride, a jog around the block, or just a walk to the end of the drive and back, do something to bring you to a fully wakeful state.

    4. Write down what you experience, where your mind wanders, everything.

    5. Repeat this for five days in a row, no breaks, and then analyze what you have written. Look for specific objectives you might want to undertake. Scribble down ideas and benchmarks for accomplishing one or more of the suggestions that crossed your mind in this week.

Now, with this renewed understanding and idea about what you want to do, what you hope to accomplish, commit to steps one to five for the next five weeks. Choose benchmarks, and begin to see yourself accomplishing more than ever. At the end of those five weeks, it will be apparent to you whether the Five AM Club is right for you. I believe you will be with us for life, from that point on.

To hear about Michael's new books first (and to be notified when there are free promotions), sign up to his New Release Mailing List.

Finally, if you enjoyed this book, please take the time to share your thoughts and post a review on Amazon. It'd be greatly appreciated!

Thank you and good luck!

Preview Of 'The 5 AM Club: 11 Tips To Help You Wake Up Early, Energize And Get Things Done' by Michael Lombardi

CHAPTER 1: HELPING YOU TO FIND THE MOTIVATION YOU NEED TO WAKE UP EARLY

The goal of this chapter is to help you answer the three most important questions that you are probably asking yourself:

1. How frustrated do you feel by the fact that you are unable to wake up in the morning?

2. Why would it benefit you to learn about why you cannot wake up in the morning?

3. Why is the reason that you would want to learn how to wake up early in the morning?

Let's take it slow and answer each question in sections.

1. Frustration

Now when you think of your frustration, it is best to actually think about how frustrated you really are. So, it is best to see how frustrated you are on a scale of 1 to 10.

1-4: In this range you do not feel frustrated at all. In your mind the fact that you cannot wake up in the morning is even a problem.

5: At this point you will feel slightly frustrated and feel annoyed about this from time to time.

6-10: At this point you are so frustrated with not being able to wake up in the morning that it actually may bring you to tears. You may feel a feeling of rage and want to scream at the world for this frustration.

If you are frustrated in the range that is lower than 6, I will not be able to do anything to help you with this problem. Why is this?

It is simply because changing anybody's habits is a true struggle in the first place, even if it is something that they want to do. When you try to do something that you are not passionate about, this makes the process almost impossible to accomplish.

Having your emotions in line with what you truly want to do is a good sign and it is something that you should have. The more important it is for you to want to wake up early every morning, the more likely it will be that you will be able to achieve this in the long run. The more you want it, the more that you are willing to do to make this change.

That is where the frustration you are feeling will come into play. It will be your main driving force behind this and will actually help you to push forward and get exactly what you want.

Now, in order to do this you will need to make yourself aware of how frustrated you really are and actually increase that frustration. It is a good idea to focus on the negative aspects of what you are lacking, so you can achieve your main goal in the long run. To do this ask yourself these important questions:

1. Do you often feeling tired all of the time? Does this feeling of being tired radiate throughout your entire body?

2. Do you wake up so late that you cannot even take a shower before heading out for the day?

3. Do you want to wake up early so you can avoid being late to work?

4. Do you want to wake up early so you can have more time to work on the projects that you need to work on?

Once you work on answering these questions, it is time to actually get to work. So, I have an assignment for you:

Assignment

Make a list of the different reasons why waking up later rather than earlier is a very bad thing for you. Think of things such as being late to work or waking up with not enough time on your hands.

2. Joy

When you decide to change a habit of yours, one of the most important things that you will need is self-discipline. Remember, in order to change a habit, you need to be motivated and the overall success of that change is figuring out how motivated you are. Once you have uncovered your motivation, then your self-discipline will set in. Remember, if you try to focus this self-discipline in a way that you do not want to do, you will end up destroying your self-confidence and will to change.

You can already see what kind of frustration you suffer from when you are unable to get up. Use that to your advantage and motivate yourself to do something about it. This is where joy can come into play. Use the joy you feel when you think about waking up early and being more productive and use that to help yourself to become motivated as well.

So, think about what is positive about getting up in the morning? What will come out of it that will make you happy?

In order to experience the joy for yourself, you need to toss out any negative thoughts of what may happen if you do not reach your goal. In order to be successful you need to think only about the positive aspects, not the negative.

So, time for your second assignment.

Assignment

Make a list of the many things that you can think of as positive about learning how to get up early in the morning and what positive things will happen to you if you wake up in the morning.

As you write this list imagine how your life will dramatically change by waking up early in the morning. Will your life change in anyway? Will you feel better about yourself and why? What would be different in your life? Why do you want to wake up early in the morning?

3. Why?

Now, if you have found the many reasons you need to change something in your life, you will succeed much more than those who walk around without a clear sense of direction to reach their goal. This is the whole point of the questions I have asked you to ask yourself in the beginning of the chapter. This will help give you a strong sense of your overall goal and help you to find the motivation that you need to reach your goal.

And now it is time for your third assignment.

Assignment

Make another list filled with at least 20 different reasons as to why you want to learn how to wake up early in the morning. While you make this list, keep in mind a few tips that will make it easier.

1. Make sure that when you create this list you are absolutely sure of the reasons that you have chosen. This will help you to dig much deeper into your true motivation and will help you to succeed in the long run.

2. Hang this list somewhere you will be able to see it often. This will help you to remind yourself of your long-term goal and will help when you are feeling as if you are failing.

Click here to check out the rest of The 5 AM Club: 11 Tips To Help You Wake Up Early, Energize And Get Things Done on Amazon.

Or go to: http://amzn.to/1CKwBk2

If the links do not work, for whatever reason, you can simply search for the pen name of the author or the name of the titles on the Amazon website to find them.

More Books for Self Help Readers

Click here to check out the rest of Michael Lombardi's books on Amazon.

Below you'll find some of my other popular books that are popular on Amazon and Kindle as well. Simply click on the links below to check them out. Alternatively, you can visit my author page on Amazon to see other work done by me.

How To Be Unstoppable Every Day Of Your Life

Mindset Manifesto: 37 Habits That Will Improve Happiness, Diminish Stress and Accelerate Peak Performance (The Power Of Mindset)

The 5 AM Club: How To Get More Done While The World Is Sleeping

The 5 AM Club: 11 Tips To Help You Wake Up Early, Energize And Get Things Done

Daily Routines: 30 Days To Achieve Enormous Gains In Life, Love And Happiness With Simple Daily Habits

If the links do not work, for whatever reason, you can simply search for these titles on the Amazon website to find them.

Printed in the USA
CPSIA information can be obtained
at www.ICGtesting.com
LVHW020057190224
772197LV00009B/943